GREEN PLANET
SOLAR POWER

by Rebecca Pettiford

pogo

Ideas for Parents and Teachers

Pogo Books let children practice reading informational text while introducing them to nonfiction features such as headings, labels, sidebars, maps, and diagrams, as well as a table of contents, glossary, and index.

Carefully leveled text with a strong photo match offers early fluent readers the support they need to succeed.

Before Reading

- "Walk" through the book and point out the various nonfiction features. Ask the student what purpose each feature serves.
- Look at the glossary together. Read and discuss the words.

Read the Book

- Have the child read the book independently.
- Invite him or her to list questions that arise from reading.

After Reading

- Discuss the child's questions. Talk about how he or she might find answers to those questions.
- Prompt the child to think more. Ask: Think of all the buildings you spend time in on a regular basis. Do any of them use solar power?

Pogo Books are published by Jump!
5357 Penn Avenue South
Minneapolis, MN 55419
www.jumplibrary.com

Copyright © 2017 Jump!
International copyright reserved in all countries. No part of this book may be reproduced in any form without written permission from the publisher.

Library of Congress Cataloging-in-Publication Data

Names: Pettiford, Rebecca, author.
Title: Solar power / by Rebecca Pettiford.
Description: Minneapolis, MN: Jump!, Inc., [2016]
Series: Green planet | Audience: Ages 7-10.
Includes bibliographical references and index.
Identifiers: LCCN 2016017103 (print)
LCCN 2016017721 (ebook)
ISBN 9781620314043 (hardcover: alk. paper)
ISBN 9781624964510 (ebook)
Subjects: LCSH: Solar energy—Juvenile literature.
Renewable energy Sources—Juvenile literature.
Classification: LCC TJ810.3 .P486 2016 (print)
LCC TJ810.3 (ebook) | DDC 621.31/244—dc23
LC record available at https://lccn.loc.gov/2016017103

Series Editor: Jenny Fretland VanVoorst
Series Designer: Anna Peterson
Book Designer: Leah Sanders
Photo Researcher: Kirsten Chang

Photo Credits: Alamy, 14-15, 20-21; Getty, 6-7, 10-11; iStock, 18-19; Shutterstock, 3, 4, 5, 9, 16-17, 23; Superstock, 8; Thinkstock, cover, 1, 12-13, 17.

Printed in the United States of America at Corporate Graphics in North Mankato, Minnesota.

TABLE OF CONTENTS

CHAPTER 1

. . . .

THE POWER OF THE SUN

Every day the sun shines down on Earth. It floods the planet with energy in the form of heat and light.

This energy is free. It will never run out. We can use this power to heat air and water. We can use it to cook food. We can turn it into electricity to power our TV and lights.

Solar power is good for the **environment**. It does not make **pollution**. It is a **renewable resource**. So how does it work?

CHAPTER 2

COLLECTORS AND CELLS

For thousands of years people have used the sun to heat their buildings. The ancient Romans put large windows in their bathhouses to trap the sun's heat. Even in winter, the buildings stayed warm.

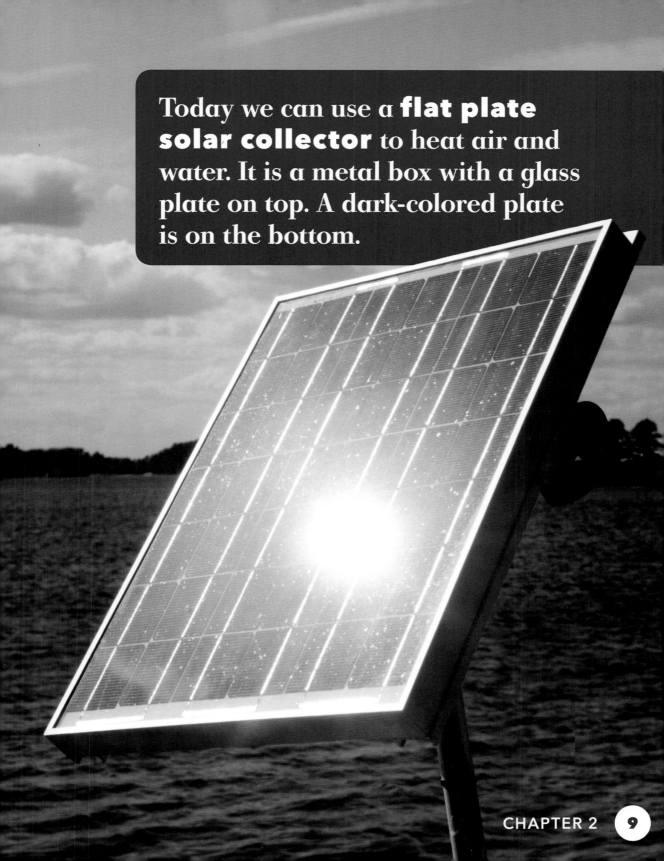

Today we can use a **flat plate solar collector** to heat air and water. It is a metal box with a glass plate on top. A dark-colored plate is on the bottom.

Sunlight passes through the glass plate. It hits the dark plate. The dark plate gets hot. It heats the air or water inside the collector.

Now we can heat the air in our home. We can take a hot bath.

Have you ever seen a roof with **solar panels** on it? Each panel is made up of **solar cells**. The cells change the sun's light to electricity.

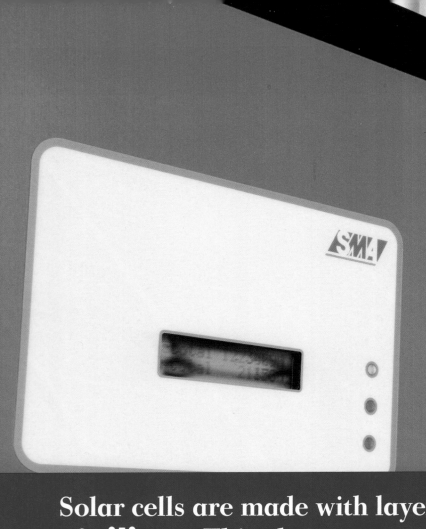

inverter

Solar cells are made with layers of **silicon**. This element reacts with the sun's rays. It creates an electrical current. Cells send the electricity to an **inverter**. It changes the current. Now it can be used in your home. You can heat water. You can turn on lights. You can watch TV.

TAKE A LOOK!

What does a home need to change the sun's energy into electricity?

① **Solar Panel**
② **Solar Cell**
③ **Inverter**
④ **Breaker or Fuse Box**

CHAPTER 3

PROBLEMS AND BENEFITS

Solar power has some problems. To make enough power, we may need many cells. This can cost a lot of money.

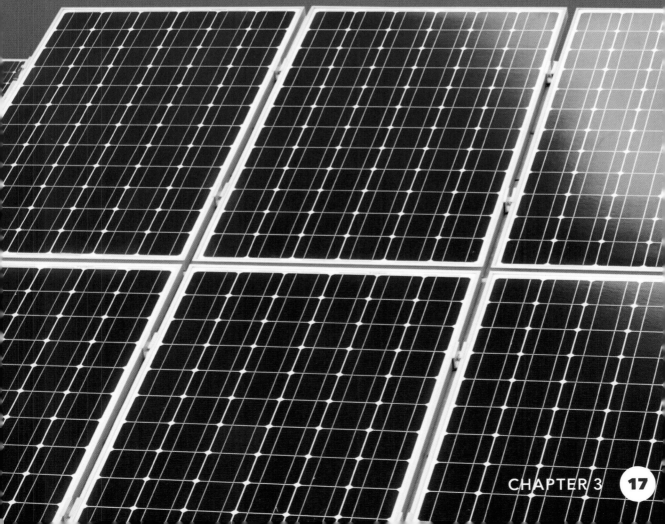

The amount of sunlight we get changes. When it is dark or cloudy, we cannot make much power.

But the benefits are great. Solar power helps fight **global warming**. More electricity made from the sun's energy means power plants will burn less coal. They will release less **greenhouse gas**.

Solar power also creates jobs. As more of us use it, we will need more workers to set up the systems.

DID YOU KNOW?

Earth gets more energy from the sun in one hour than its people use in a year!

solar cooker

Solar power is already a big part of our lives. From **solar cookers** to sun-heated pools, there are many ways to use the sun's power. How do you use the sun?

DID YOU KNOW?

In some countries, people use the sun to cook food. There is no need to burn wood. Solar cookers use dark surfaces to absorb heat. They use shiny surfaces to direct the sun's light.

ACTIVITIES & TOOLS

TRY THIS!

HEAT PIZZA IN A SOLAR COOKER

Trap the sun's heat in a box to warm a slice of pizza.

What You Need:

- an empty pizza box with a lid that closes
- aluminum foil
- plastic wrap
- tape
- scissors
- ruler
- paper plate
- a leftover pizza slice

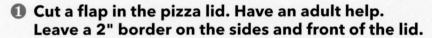

❶ Cut a flap in the pizza lid. Have an adult help. Leave a 2" border on the sides and front of the lid.

❷ Wrap the bottom side of the flap and the inside bottom of the box with foil, shiny side out. Tape in place.

❸ Cover the opening made by the flap with plastic wrap. Tape in place. It should be tight.

❹ Put a cold pizza slice on a paper plate. Put it inside the oven. Close the lid tightly.

❺ Prop open the flap with a ruler. Move the box so that the sun shines off the foil into the cooker.

❻ Let the sun heat the pizza. Depending on how hot it is, this could take up to an hour.

❼ Remove the slice. Be careful. The pizza may be hot!

GLOSSARY

environment: The surroundings or conditions in which a person, animal, or plant lives.

flat plate solar collector: A device that has a flat glass or plastic plate with dark metal surfaces that take in or collect solar energy.

global warming: A warming of Earth's environment.

greenhouse gas: Gas that collects in the atmosphere, trapping heat close to Earth's surface and promoting global warming.

inverter: A device that changes direct current to alternating current.

pollution: Something harmful that is in the environment.

renewable resource: A supply of something natural that is easily replaced.

silicon: One of the most common elements in Earth's crust; it is often used in electronic devices.

solar cells: Devices that change the sun's light energy to electricity.

solar cooker: A device that uses the sun's heat to cook food.

solar panels: Flat devices that are made up of solar cells.

solar power: Energy from the sun that is changed into electricity or heat.

INDEX

TO LEARN MORE

Learning more is as easy as 1, 2, 3.

1) Go to www.factsurfer.com

2) Enter "solarpower" into the search box.

3) Click the "Surf" button to see a list of websites.

With factsurfer, finding more information is just a click away.